Shapes

Library of Congress Number: 79-19852

   3 4 5 6 7 8 9 0 83 82 81

Printed in the United States of America.

Library of Congress Cataloging in Publication Data

Allington, Richard L
  Shapes.

  (Beginning to learn about)
  SUMMARY: Introduces 20 geometric figures with
activities involving shapes and size relationships.
  1. Form perception — Juvenile literature. 2. Size
perception — Juvenile literature. [1. Size and shape.
2. Geometry] I. Ehlert, Lois. II. Title.
III. Series.
BF293.A44   153.7′52   79-19852
ISBN 0-8172-1277-9 lib. bdg.

Richard L. Allington is Associate Professor, Department of Reading,
State University of New York at Albany

BEGINNING TO LEARN ABOUT

SHAPES

BY RICHARD L. ALLINGTON, PH. D. •

Raintree Childrens Books · Milwaukee

circle

A circle is round.

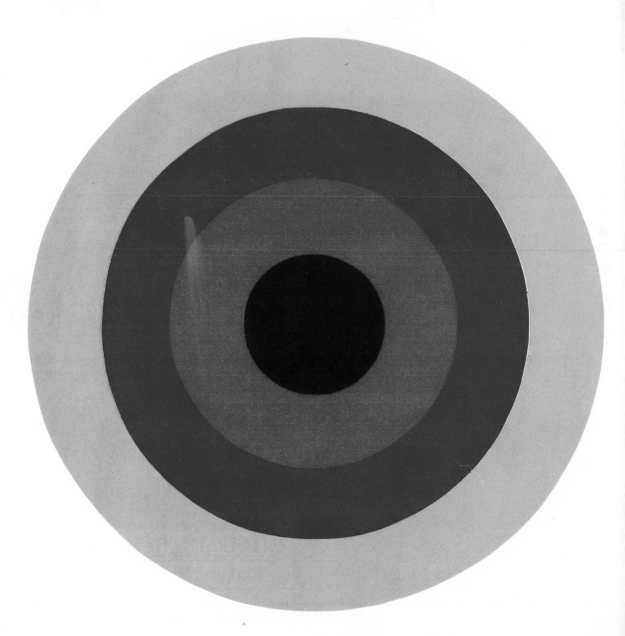

4

Which circles will the black circle cover?

square

A square has 4 sides of the same length

2

1

3

4

6

Find the biggest square.

triangle

A triangle has 3 sides.

1

2

3

Find the smallest triangle.

rectangle

A rectangle has 4 sides.

2

1

4

Which is the longest rectangle?

Which is the shortest?

star

These stars have 5 points.

Which stars are the same size?

oval

An oval is shaped like an egg.

Which is the largest oval?

Which is the littlest?

pentagon

A pentagon has 5 sides.

Which is the smallest pentagon?

17

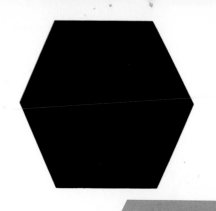

hexagon

A hexagon has 6 sides.

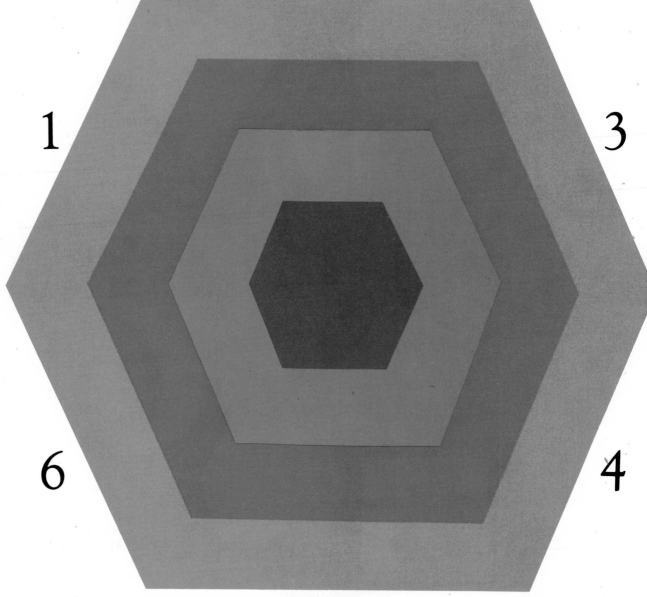

1

2

3

4

5

6

Find the 8 hexagons in this picture.

Which is the biggest hexagon?

Which is the smallest hexagon?

19

heptagon

A heptagon has 7 sides.

Which heptagons will the black heptagon cover?

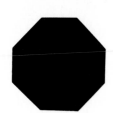

octagon

An octagon has 8 sides.

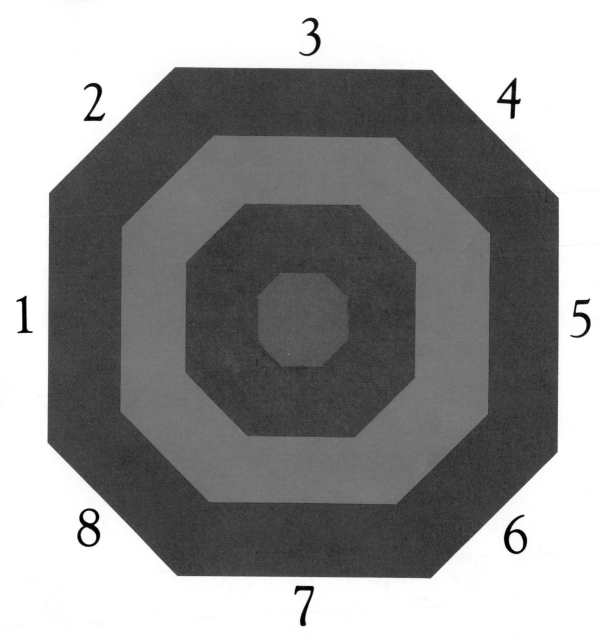

Which octagons are
bigger than the
green octagons?

Here are some
other shapes.

Find the biggest shape in each row.

sphere

cube

pyramid

cone

cylinder

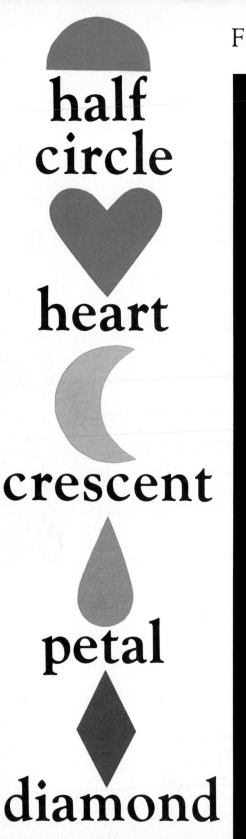

half
circle

heart

crescent

petal

diamond

Which shapes will cover the mouse?

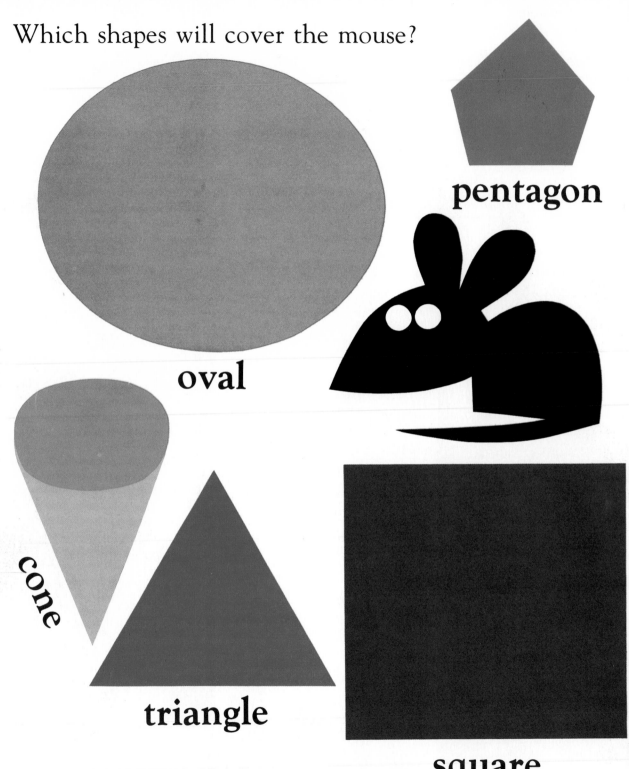

oval

pentagon

cone

triangle

square

Which animals will fit inside the octagon?

With your finger, draw a line from each word to the shape that matches.

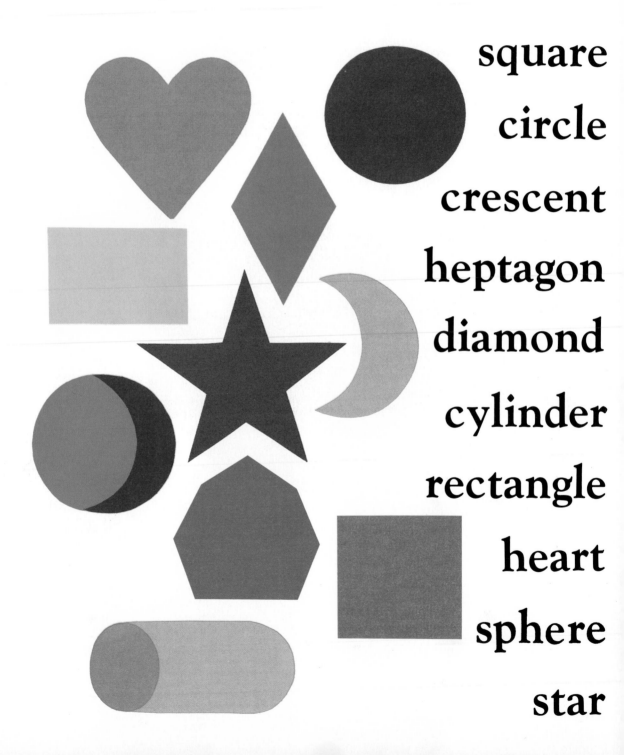

square

circle

crescent

heptagon

diamond

cylinder

rectangle

heart

sphere

star

cube

triangle

pyramid

petal

pentagon

cone

hexagon

octagon

oval

half circle

How many shapes can you find in this picture?
What are they?

Start your own collection of shapes. Find things or pictures of things that are the same shape as the shapes in this book. For example, find a clock or ball to match the circle shape. See how many different shapes you can find.